STRING INSTRUMENTS

Purchasing, Maintenance,
Troubleshooting,
and More

SANDY GOLDIE

Published by
Meredith Music Publications
a division of G.W. Music, Inc.
1584 Estuary Trail, Delray Beach, Florida 33483
http://www.meredithmusic.com

MEREDITH MUSIC PUBLICATIONS and its stylized double M logo are trademarks of
MEREDITH MUSIC PUBLICATIONS, a division of G.W. Music, Inc.

Text and cover design: Shawn Girsberger

International Standard Book Number: 978-1-57463-056-5
Cataloging-in-Publication Data is on file with the Library of Congress.
Library of Congress Control Number: 2017909507
Printed and bound in U.S.A.

CONTENTS

ACKNOWLEDGEMENTS

Because this book represents the collective wisdom and perspective of many well-respected orchestra and string teachers across the country, I am greatly indebted to the many directors, friends and teachers whose valuable ideas and contributions are represented in this book:

> My great mentor and friend, **Charles West**, who originally put the idea of writing this book in my head.

> The most amazing peer editor, partner-in-crime, and content analyst for all things strings, **Susanna Klein**, Assistant Professor of Violin and Coordinator or Strings at Virginia Commonwealth University and President of VASTA. The influence of her professional and personal support during the process of writing this book cannot be over-stated.

> **Jacob Dakon**, Assistant Professor of Music Education at Kansas State University, for his contributions on string instrument renting and purchasing.

> **The dedicated and hard-working School Orchestra and String Teachers all around the country** who shared their experiences and knowledge with me directly and as part of the ongoing conversations in the Facebook Group: *School Orchestra and String Teachers* created by **Gail Barnes** at the University of SC. I thank you all, not just for what you contributed to this work, but to the ongoing and important work you do each and every day that makes so much difference in the lives of children and in the life of our society that is in such desperate need of that which only music education has to offer. May you never underestimate the value of the work you do.

A special thank you to the following teachers:

>*Seth Gamba, Bassist, String Pedagogy Author, and Public School Orchestra Teacher, Fulton County, GA*

>*Margaret Selby, Public School Orchestra Teacher, SCMEA and SC ASTA Leadership, Charleston, SC*

>*Kelly Ali, Bass Instructor at VCU Music and Bassist, Richmond Symphony Orchestra, Richmond, VA*

>*Matt Gold, Bassist, Richmond Symphony Orchestra, Richmond, VA*

>*Christopher Selby, nationally-recognized String Pedagogy Author, NAfME and SCMEA Leadership, and Public School Orchestra Teacher, Charleston SC*

>*Catherine Bond, Jennifer Herrera, and Laura Thomas, Public School Orchestra Teachers, Virginia Schools*

I also thank my loving husband, **Amos Goldie,** *whose selfless help and love are etched into the crevices of each of these chapters* as well as **Garwood Whaley**, my editor at Meredith Music Publications, whose valuable insights, skillful editing, and hours of effort have formed and shaped these ideas into a usable finished product that I believe will be the most valuable and well-organized resource that it can be for helping string teachers and players successfully purchase, maintain and solve problems related to the string instruments they cherish and use to maintain their livelihoods. Without Gar's recognition that this book is as vitally important for string players as the others in the series are for woodwind, brass, and percussionists, the project would still be just a wish.

INTRODUCTION

Over the past twenty-five years, I've had the pleasure of working alongside so many great orchestra teachers, studio teachers, professional string players and string students. I cannot help but to recall the many conversations over the years about the kinds of problems that we repeatedly encounter while teaching and playing string instruments as well as the creative (and sometimes comical) solutions we have found to remedy them—everything from slipping pegs and sticking endpins to faulty equipment and bows that will no longer tighten. Of course, all of these happen at the most convenient time (never just before the performance) and our budgets are all bursting with funds for repair! Even after many years of playing and teaching string instruments, many of us readily admit that we wish we knew more about specific aspects of string instrument purchase, maintenance and trouble-shooting.

After interviewing many colleagues for this book (see acknowledgements), I realized that we each possess some bits of knowledge that are valuable pieces of the puzzle. It became apparent to me that so many of us want to share what we know with each other and to learn from others if only given a forum to do so. This book is my sincere attempt to do just that and to share (from one orchestra teacher to others in the profession) the collection of things I have learned over a lifetime of playing and teaching in hopes that it might benefit you and your students. By summarizing the collective wisdom shared with me by colleagues across the profession, I hope that you might gain (as I have) a deeper understanding of the things that can help us and our students do what we do more successfully.

I dedicate this book to each of you, *the hard-working public school orchestra teachers* out there making a difference in student's lives every day through the power of string music education. Never doubt that what you do makes a difference and changes the world—one child at a time. May what you find in this book help you in that journey!

STRINGS IN GENERAL: PROBLEMS AND SOLUTIONS APPLICABLE TO ALL STRING INSTRUMENTS

Instrument Selection and Sizing

String instruments come in many different sizes (see the following chart); therefore, it is possible for students of any size to play any string instrument (violin, viola cello, bass). Students generally do best when allowed to select their own instrument and then the appropriate size of that instrument is matched to their arm length and hand span. For cellos and basses, height must also be considered. Students should be measured carefully so that they never play a string instrument that is too large for them. Below are guidelines for measuring:

- **Violin/Viola** (Measure 2 Things)

  1. *Left Arm Length* from the end of the shoulder to the end of the middle finger when the arm is stretched out straight. Be sure there is no bend in the elbow.

  2. *Left Hand Span* from the tip of the left index finger to the tip of the pinky finger when the fingers are spread apart as far as possible.

     » Note: To play a full size, both the student's arm AND the hand span must be large enough (see the following chart). If there is a conflict between sizes, always go with the smaller size.

- **Cello/Bass** (Measure 3 Things)

  1. *Left Arm Length* from the end of the right shoulder to the end of the middle finger when the arm is stretched out straight. Be sure there is no bend in the elbow.

  2. *Left Hand Span* from the tip of the left index finger to the tip of the pinky finger when the fingers are spread apart as far as possible.

3. *Height* from the top of the head to the ground when standing up straight wearing flat shoes (no heels).

 » Note: To play the largest size, the student must meet full size criteria for all three categories (see the following chart). If there is a conflict between sizes, always go with the smallest size category.

■ *Instrument Sizing Chart*

Chart to be used for selecting correct sized instruments for students

	Size	Left hand span	Left arm length	Height
Violin	Full	over 5 inches	over 24 inches	Not important
	3/4	4½–5 inches	21–24 inches	
	1/2	4–4½ inches	18–21 inches	
	1/4	3½–4 inches	under 18 inches	
Viola	16 inch	over 6 inches	over 28 inches	Not important
	15½ inch	6 inches	26 inches	
	15 inch	5½ inches	25 inches	
	14 inch	5 inches	24 inches	
	13¼ inch	4½ inches	21 inches	
Cello	Full	6 inches	24 inches	60 inches
	3/4	5 inches	22 inches	56 inches
	1/2	4 inches	20 inches	52 inches
	1/4	3 inches	18 inches	48 inches
Bass	3/4	6½ inches	24 inches	60 inches
	1/2	5¾ inches	22 inches	56 inches
	1/4	5 inches	20 inches	52 inches

■ *Warning!* It is better for an instrument to be too small than too large. Assign the instrument according to the smallest category size and re-measure yearly. Playing an instrument that is too large can cause:

 • physical injury

 • improper playing techniques

 • faulty intonation (cannot reach proper finger spacing)

 • limited tone production (cannot reach all portions of the bow)

Additional Notes:

- All string instruments come in fractional sizes except for violas, which are sized by inches. Any viola longer than 15½ inches is considered the full size.

- ¾ Bass is considered the largest size (see chart above).

- If a student is not big enough for a junior viola, they can start on a ½ size violin strung with viola strings. A 13.5 inch viola is the same size as a ¾ size violin.

Instrument Diagrams

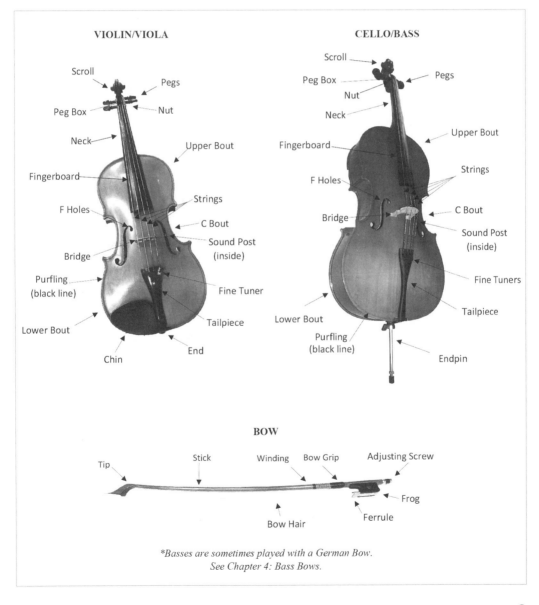

VIOLIN/VIOLA

Scroll
Pegs
Peg Box
Nut
Neck
Upper Bout
Fingerboard
Strings
F Holes
C Bout
Bridge
Sound Post (inside)
Purfling (black line)
Fine Tuner
Lower Bout
Tailpiece
Chin
End

CELLO/BASS

Scroll
Peg Box
Pegs
Nut
Neck
Upper Bout
Fingerboard
Strings
F Holes
Bridge
C Bout
Sound Post (inside)
Fine Tuners
Tailpiece
Lower Bout
Purfling (black line)
Endpin

BOW

Tip
Stick
Winding
Bow Grip
Adjusting Screw
Frog
Ferrule
Bow Hair

*Basses are sometimes played with a German Bow.
See Chapter 4: Bass Bows.*

Instrument Care and Maintenance

Proper maintenance and storage are crucial for protecting the value, beauty, functionality and sound of a string instrument. There are some things you should do daily (each time you play), other things you should check periodically and a few things that should be done annually. Below are some tips and checklists for properly caring for your instrument:

■ Daily Instrument and Bow Care

Instrument Care
Do the following each time you play the instrument:

- Wipe off the strings and wood after playing with a soft, dry cloth to remove all rosin, dirt, and fingerprints.

- Handle the instrument gently (by the neck) while taking it in and out of the case to prevent scratches and damage to wood and bridge.

- Unpack with the case flat on the floor to prevent falling and breakage.

- Be sure the instrument is stored in the case properly and that the case is securely latched/zipped before picking it up. Violins and Violas must remove shoulder pads before storage.

- Put the endpin in any time the instrument is not being played (cello/bass).

- Always keep your instrument in the case when it is not in use.

Do not:

- Hang the instrument on a music stand or leave it on the floor or chair unattended.

- Lay the instrument on its side with the endpin out or walk around with the endpin out (cello/bass). Doing so can cause injury as well as expensive damage to the bridge and wood.

Bow Care
Do the following each time you play the instrument:

- Loosen the bow after each use.

- Tighten the bow hair before playing.

Do not:

- Touch the bow hair. Finger oils damage them and they will no longer hold rosin.

- Loosen it so much that it falls out of the stick (see the following diagram).

■ *Warning!* Failure to loosen the bow can stretch out the hair and warp the stick.

Too Tight (stick straightens)

Proper Tension (stick is curved)

Loosened When Not Playing

Temperature and Moisture Control

Temperature

■ Keep the instrument at a relatively consistent temperature (60–75 degrees). Avoid rapid changes and any extreme heat or cold. The glue holding the instrument together can melt in the heat or the wood can crack from the cold. In general, never leave your instrument any place where you (or your new puppy) would not be comfortable.

Moisture

■ Strive to keep the instrument at a relatively consistent humidity year-round in order to avoid cracks in the wood (30%–55% humidity). Consider using a humidifier in your house or school during winter months or purchasing an in-instrument humidifier for the instrument if necessary.

Warning!

■ Do not let the instrument get wet. Moisture damages the varnish. Always transport the instrument inside of the case if outdoors.

■ *Never leave the instrument in the car!*

■ Periodic Maintenance

Bridge

Keep an eye on the bridge regularly!

The bridge is positioned correctly if: 1. the strings are centered over the fingerboard, 2. the bridge is at a 90 degree angle to the instrument, and 3. the bridge is aligned with the notches of the f hole (see diagram below).

Check the Placement

■ If the bridge gets bumped, it may move small amounts since it is not (and should not be) glued down. Try not to bump this part of the instrument because it can break, fall down and/or crack the top of the instrument.

Check the Angle

■ As you tune the instrument, the strings tend to pull the top of the bridge towards the fingerboard. If the bridge leans too far forward and falls over, it can break and even crack the wood on top of the instrument. If the bridge is cracked or broken, the sound post inside of the instrument can also fall down. Never play an instrument with the sound post down. Loosen the string tension and put the instrument away immediately and take it to a qualified string repair person.

Adjust

■ If the bridge is not positioned correctly, it can be carefully adjusted with two hands by a trained teacher or qualified repair person by pinching the base of the bridge between the thumbs and index fingers on each hand and making small micro-adjustments. It is helpful to loosen some tension from the stings before doing this. If you loosen all tension from all strings, the bridge will fall over.

Proper Angle: 90°   Leaning

Proper Placement

Misaligned

Reposition with 2 Hands

Fine Tuners

Keep an eye on the fine tuners regularly!

- ■ *Check*. Check the screw on each fine tuner to be sure it hasn't been tightened so much that the wood underneath is being scratched (see diagram below).

- ■ *Repair or Replace*. Repair any fine tuner that won't turn easily (see Chapter 2: Broken or Malfunctioning Fine Tuners). Replace fine tuners that are broken or stripped out.

Yes!

No!

Fine tuner is scratching wood.

■ *Annual Maintenance*

- ■ Perform the following maintenance yearly (more often if possible):

Wood

- ■ *Clean and Polish*. Deep clean and polish the instrument with a soft cloth to remove built up rosin and dirt and protect the finish. I recommend Kohlstein's All-Instrument Cleaner and Polish. ***WARNING:*** *Never use any type of cleaner or polish on your instrument that isn't designed specifically for string instruments! Do not apply water or any kind of furniture polish to your instrument.* Follow these steps:
  - ● *Step 1*. Wipe off surface level rosin with a soft, dry cloth made of non-abrasive material such as cotton or microfiber.

- *Step 2.* Apply a cleaner *made specifically for string instruments* to the cloth. Wipe down all of the wood, rubbing in the direction of the grain (top to bottom for the front of the instrument, for example). Be sure to apply the cleaner to the cloth, not directly to the instrument.

- *Step 3.* Apply a small amount of polish *made specifically for string instruments* to a separate soft cloth. Rub the cloth into the wood using a small circular motion. Work the polish into all areas of the wood evenly. Use a separate cloth to wipe off any excess polish.

Strings

- *Check.* Check each string to be sure it is not cutting into the bridge; especially, the violin E string and viola A string (see diagram below). This often occurs if the small rubber piece is not aligned properly with the groove on the bridge. This piece can be repositioned by loosening the string and sliding it to the correct location.

- *Replace.* Replace strings that are broken, false or fraying. For instructions, see Chapter 2: Troubleshooting and Repair: Strings.

Prevents string from cutting into bridge

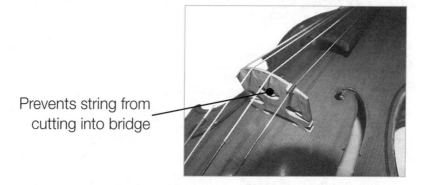

Bows

- *Rehair.* Have the bow rehaired once a year if financially feasible. Do this sooner if the hair is thinning (missing many hairs), stretched out (won't tighten properly), or warn out (won't produce a consistent tone).

- *Repair.* Send bows off for repair if they will not tighten or loosen easily.

- *Replace.* Replace bows with warped sticks (see diagram below).

Warped Bow as seen from above

Not Warped

Fingerboards

■ *Clean.* The fingerboard (and strings) can be cleaned by putting a very small amount of rubbing alcohol or denatured alcohol on a clean, dry cloth and wiping the surface. ***WARNING:*** Alcohol will damage any varnish it comes in contact with so use the bare minimum needed and be very careful that it does not drip on the wood.

Endpins

■ *Check.* Check the endpin for each cello and bass and have it repaired if it is slipping or stuck in place. See Chapter 4: Troubleshooting and Repair—Endpin.

Cases

■ *Check.* Check that each case zips completely and latches properly. Also, be sure the mechanism inside of the case that holds the bow in place is functioning properly so that the bow does not fall out and scratch the top of the instrument.

■ *Replace.* Replacing cases that are worn out or won't close properly sooner rather than later can prevent costly damage to instruments

Instrument Storage and Procedures

Many instruments are damaged each year due to poor or inadequate instrument storage space or improper storage procedures. To avoid costly damage and repairs, consider the following:

Individual Instruments

■ Violin/Viola—see Chapter 2

■ Cello—see Chapter 3

■ Bass—see Chapter 4

Classroom Storage

■ Maintain Consistent Temperature and Moisture Control (see above).

■ Install Instrument Storage Racks

   ● When selecting the best instrument storage to fit your needs, three things are important to consider: 1. budget and logistics, 2. ample bridge and bow protection, and 3. importance of placement.

      1. *Budget and Logistics.* Take into account the amount of space you have, number of instruments, and how much your school will allow you to spend. I recommend the following:

- Wenger String Instrument Storage custom fit to your space for all instruments.

$$ Moderate Budget:

- Upper Strings: folding tables marked clearly with student names (or assigned numbers)

- Lower Strings: Pre-made Wenger Cello and Bass Storage Cabinets.

$ Small Budget:

- Upper Strings: folding tables marked clearly with student names (or assigned numbers)

- Lower Strings: Assemble cello and bass racks yourself (or with a handy parent) made of either PVC Piping or wood that can be purchased at any home improvement store. Plans for this can be found online at the School Orchestra Teachers Facebook group.

2. *Ample Bridge and Bow Protection.* However you structure your storage, it must provide protection for both the bridge and the bow of instruments that are in soft cases. Violins and violas generally come in hard cases so this is mostly an issue for cellos and basses.

- *Bridge.* Each cello and bass should be held upright so that the bridge of one instrument does not touch another instrument or lean against a wall. The bridge is very fragile and is not designed to hold weight.

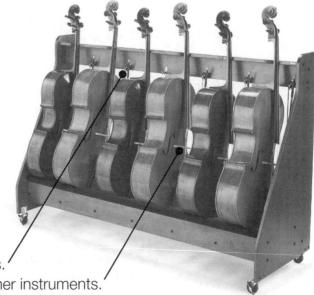

- Hooks for cello/bass bows.
- Bridges do not contact other instruments.

- *Bow.* Bows should be stored inside of instrument cases unless using specifically designed cello/bass racks that hold instruments without the cases (suggested). The safest place for a bow if not in the case is hanging on a sturdy hook by the frog.

3. *Importance of Placement.* Carefully map out the desired student traffic patterns in your space before deciding on placement for storage racks. Here are some guiding principles:

- Try to locate storage for each instrument closest to that instrument's rehearsal position in the room.

- Avoid overlapping traffic patterns such as violins walking through the cello section to store instruments.

- Spread out instrument storage to different areas of the room to limit the congregation of large crowds in one location. The more crowded any one location is, the more likely an instrument will get bumped, dropped or damaged.

■ Establish Proper Instrument Storage and Handling Procedures

- Even with high quality instrument storage racks in place, many instruments will still get damaged if proper procedures are not well-established in the classroom. Creating proactive, effective instrument procedures can prevent costly accidents. Students should be specifically trained to prevent damage to instruments and injury to each other. All storage should be assigned and labeled clearly.

  » *Assignments*

  - Have each cello/bass student assigned to one specific instrument and bow to use daily. Not allowing students to switch instruments at will is both financially and pedagogically sound (different size necks play differently). This makes it clear that each student is responsible for the care/damage of that one instrument during their class. Keep an accurate list of who plays each instrument in each class to make it easy to follow-up on maintenance issues. Sometimes allowing students to select and name the instrument also helps!

  - Assign each student one storage location for their instrument (that they can reach easily). This prevents arguing over spaces, damage to equipment, and racing to premium locations.

» *Training*

- The importance of student training for preventing instrument damage cannot be over-stated. Have each section practice the storage routine under teacher supervision. Demonstrate what is and is not acceptable as far as: 1. loosening bows/wiping off rosin/putting in endpins, 2. horsing around or congregating in storage areas, 3. placing the instrument gently and carefully in storage and what it should (and should not) look like in the cabinet/table/rack when stored properly.

- *Contracts*

  » For school-owned instruments, have students and parents sign an "Instrument Use Contract" (see Appendix) to establish clear expectations for care and handling as well as financial responsibility for damages caused by inappropriate use or neglect. Large instruments (cellos and basses) should not be transported on a school bus, bicycle or motorcycle.

- *Starting Rehearsal*

  » The first five minutes and last five minutes of class or rehearsal are the times when the most instrument damage occurs. Be proactive to help prevent student injury and costly instrument repairs. Be sure students know exactly where and how to unpack instrument cases in such a way that there are clear paths (see Appendix diagram) to walk without tripping over cases or stepping on instruments and bows. I suggest having each student unpack with their case flat on the floor at their own chair. Store violin/viola cases standing up between pairs of chairs and have cello/bass cases folded under chairs. All backpacks can be placed under chairs. Advantages to this are:

    - Clear isles prevent tripping with and on instruments during movement.

    - Unpacking at floor level prevents instruments from falling and breaking when dropped.

    - Unpacking at seats prevents congregation of large groups anywhere in the classroom that increase likelihood of horseplay, classroom management issues, delay of rehearsal start and make instrument damage more likely.

    - The safest way to transport any instrument is in the case. Instruments outside of the case during travel to and from seats increases the risk that other items (or people) damage them along the way.

- *Ending Rehearsal*
  - » When students are in a hurry to get to their next class or event, items get damaged, not cleaned, not loosened and/or not put away correctly. To avoid this, allow at least 3-5 minutes of pack-up time and consider allowing students to pack and go to storage one section at a time with the instruction to return to their seats when done.
- *During Rehearsal*
  - » Never place bows, violins or violas on the floor where they can get stepped on or dirty. Cellos and basses can be laid on their side with the endpin in for short breaks (never on the back or front of instrument). Bows should not be placed on chairs or hung from stands. It is best to lay the bow across the music stand when not in use. Do not hang violins and violas from the music stand by the scroll. It is best to create walking isles between sections and to avoid travelling through the middle of any section during breaks or other entry and exit times.

Rehearsal Space—Necessary Equipment

Below is a list of minimum equipment needed for quality string instrument rehearsal/instruction followed by selection criteria as well as their impact on string instrument maintenance and performance.

- Dedicated Strings Rehearsal Space
- Chairs/Chair Rack
- Music Stands/Stand Rack
- Conductor's Podium
- Instrument Storage Racks/Shelves
- Instructional Technology

Dedicated Strings Rehearsal Space

- It is important to have a dedicated strings-only rehearsal and storage space for both pedagogical and financial reasons. Program recruiting, retention, motivation and sense of ownership all tend to be problematic with no space to call home. Scheduling issues make extra tutoring, private lessons, help sessions and group rehearsals harder to arrange.
- The ongoing loss of instructional time (even just 5 minutes at the beginning and end of class) due to daily set-up and take-down can

represent up to a 20% loss of instructional time in a 50 minute class. Stands and chairs must be arranged differently for bands, choirs, and orchestras.

■ In addition, it is important to protect the large monetary investment in the school's string instruments and dedicated equipment. Even the most careful non-string players can cause significant damage to string instruments if they have not been properly trained in their care and protection. Often, the long-term number and cost of repairs to string instruments far exceeds the up-front cost of equipping a separate rehearsal space for orchestra.

Chairs/Chair Rack

■ Proper posture is crucial for successful string playing. Chairs should be armless. They should not roll. The seat should be flat (not bucket).

- Recommendation: Wenger Posture Chairs and matching storage rack.

- Also Acceptable: Any chair conforming to the three criteria above.

Music Stands/ Stand Rack

■ For educational purposes, it is best for each student to use their own music stand (even if they later share with a stand partner for performances). This is important for early independence training, daily monitoring that each student has the sheet music and method books necessary for home practice, and that each individual can successfully mark their own bowings and fingerings in the music they will use to practice at home. Most teachers transition to all instruments (except basses) sharing a stand as the concert approaches.

■ Wire music stands tend to fall over easily and scratch the varnish on string instruments so it is best to purchase sturdy, heavy-duty stands for daily use and reserve wire stands for emergency use, home individual practice and needed break-out sectionals. Better quality music stands are usually made of steel, aluminum, or polycarbonate materials. I recommend Manhasset Symphony or Wenger Classic with matching stand racks for storage.

Conductor's Podium

■ Choose a podium size that allows students at the back of the classroom to see all instruction, modeling and conducting.

■ Recommendation: Wenger Conductor's Podium (at least the base podium).

Instrument Storage Racks/Shelves

■ See previous section.

Stools for Basses (optional)

■ See Chapter 4: Accessories: Stools

Instructional Technology

■ Ensemble Tuner/Metronome

- Pitch and tempo stability is difficult for the ensemble to achieve without well-projected and accurate tuning pitches and metronome beats.

- Recommendation: Boss DB-90 Dr. Beat

■ Sound Amplification

- For any string group larger than 3–4 people, sound amplification is necessary for instructional audio. Amplification should be used for tuning notes, metronome work, method book accompaniment tracks, listening samples, video projection, and many other learning activities the teacher will need to use.

- Recommendation: stand-alone speakers or classroom stereo system (for the most appropriate technology for your space, contact the media or technology specialist at your institution as this technology changes rapidly).

■ Visual Display

- Several of the National Music Standards are most effectively taught (or instruction deeply enhanced) through the use of visual display.

- Recommendations: use a projector, dry erase board, SmartBoard, or Prometheus Board to display visual class content.

Troubleshooting and Repair

■ *Tuning Issues*

■ Pegs Slipping or Sticking

- *Solutions:* Try each of the following:

  » *First.* Be sure you are pushing the peg in towards the peg box as you turn. Simply turning forward will not hold the string in place.

» *Second.* Check to see if the string is wound towards the outside wall of the peg box and not the inside. If it is not, loosen the string and then wind it around the peg properly (see the following diagram).

» *Third.* If needed, place peg compound or graphite from a No. 2 pencil on the shiny grooves of the peg. Use these steps:

♦ *Step 1.* Loosen the string and pull the peg out until you can see the shiny grooves on the peg. Warning: Never remove more than one string at a time or the bridge will fall

♦ *Step 2.* Coat the shiny grooves of the peg with peg compound or graphite from a pencil. Peg compound can be purchased at your local music store or online.

♦ *Step 3.* Re-install the string (see Chapter 2: Troubleshooting: Broken String). Be sure to wind the string towards the peg wall.

» *Fourth.* If the pegs still do not function properly after doing the previous 3 steps, take the instrument to a qualified string repair person to refit the existing pegs to the openings. You can also consider replacing traditional pegs with "Perfection Pegs" that have tiny hidden gears on the inside, but are indistinguishable from traditional pegs on the outside. These work well if they are properly fitted and installed by a qualified string repair person.

String winding towards peg wall (not center)

■ Fine Tuners Malfunctioning

● *Solutions:* See Chapter 2: Troubleshooting and Repair: Strings

■ *Bow Issues*

■ Bow Will Not Tighten

● If the bow will not tighten, the environment may have become too humid causing bow hair to stretch out or the adjusting screw may be stripped out. If you are able to turn the screw, but nothing happens, it is likely stripped out due to repeatedly over-tightening the hair once it has stretched out. If the bow has not been rehaired within the last 1-2 years, this may also cause the hair to stretch.

- *Solutions:* Have a qualified repair person check the hair, screw and eyelet inside the frog. They can repair or replace as needed. In the future, maintain a relatively consistent humidity between 30-55% percent (see temperature and moisture control in maintenance section above).

  » *Warning!* Never continue to tighten the bow past the point of resistance or you will strip out the screw.

- **Bow Will Not Loosen**

  - If the bow will not loosen, the environment may be too dry causing the bow hair to shorten.

  - *Solutions:* Have a qualified repair person adjust or replace the hair and the eyelet inside the bow to solve the problem. In the future, strive to keep the humidity consistently between 30-55%.

    » *Warning!* Do not delay getting the bow to a repair shop if it will not loosen. Prolonged tension can warp the bow or cause the tip to snap right off. If this happens, you will have to replace the bow.

- **Bow Hairs Broken**

  - From time to time a bow hair may break off. If this happens occasionally, it is not cause for alarm.

  - *Solution:* Use fingernail clippers to carefully cut the one hair off at the frog or tip. Try not to damage any other hairs when cutting.

    » *Warning!* If this is happening to you repeatedly, it may mean the hair is too dry. Strive to maintain consistent humidity between 30-55 percent (see temperature and moisture control above).

- **Bow Makes No Sound**

  - *Solution:* This is normal if the bow is brand new and has never been rosined. Add rosin to the bow (for bass, travel frog to tip only). If you have used the rosin, be sure the rosin is actually coming off onto the bow. You can scratch the surface with a key to help get it started. If rosin is more than 1-2 years old (or has been melted/damaged by the sun), replace the rosin.

- **Bow Will Not Produce Consistent Tone**

  - There can be many reasons for this, but the 3 most likely causes are: 1. not enough rosin on the bow, 2. the hair is old and worn out (has not been replaced in the past 1-2 years), or 3. the stick is warped.

» *Solutions:*

- ◆ Not enough rosin: rosin the bow.

- ◆ Old or worn out hair: rehair the bow.

- ◆ Bow stick warped (see maintenance section for diagnosis diagrams). Note: You may also notice excessive wobbling of the stick when playing at the tip of the bow. Have a qualified repair person straighten or replace the bow.

» ***Warning!*** Do not continue to play on a warped bow stick. This increases the damage. If the stick cannot be straightened, it must be replaced.

■ *Bridge Issues*

■ Broken or Cracked Bridge

- ● *Solution:* If the bridge is broken or cracked, it should be replaced by a qualified string repair person who can properly fit the new bridge to the instrument.

  » ***Warning!*** Never attempt home repair of a broken or cracked bridge. Once a bridge is not structurally sound, it is likely to fall over and crack the entire top of the instrument.

■ Fallen Bridge

- ● *Solution:* If the bridge has fallen over and has not broken, it is possible to reset it in place if the sound post has not also fallen down. See previous maintenance section for positioning instructions.

  » ***Warning!*** Never use glue on any part of the bridge or the instrument. This damages the wood of the bridge and the varnish of the instrument. The bridge is held in place only by the tension of the strings. Never play an instrument with the sound post down. If you hear the sound post rattling around inside of the instrument, loosen the string tension, pack the instrument, and immediately and take it to a qualified string repair person as soon as possible to prevent cracks to the top of the instrument.

■ Bridge is Leaning or Bumped Out of Position

- ● If the bridge is leaning or has been bumped out of position, it can be repositioned *IF* it is not cracked and the sound post has not fallen.

- ● *Solution:* Reposition the bridge using 2 hands after loosening some tension from the strings (instructions in maintenance section above).

» *Warning:* Never play an instrument with the sound post down. Put it away immediately and take it to a qualified string repair person to prevent cracks to the top of the instrument.

■ *Sound Post Down*

■ Never play the instrument with the sound post down because the top of the instrument may crack. Loosen string tension and pack the instrument up immediately and take it to a qualified string repair person to reset it into the proper position. Even tiny adjustments to the placement of the sound post can dramatically impact tone on the instrument.

■ *Scratches or Cracks in the Wood*

■ *Scratches.* Small, surface-level scratches generally do not cause structural damage to the instrument and are therefore mainly cosmetic issues.

- *Solution:* Try using a high quality string instrument cleaner and polish like *Kohlstein All-Instrument.* These can sometimes make small scratches less visible (for instructions, see maintenance section above).

  » *Warning!* Never apply water, furniture polish or any cleaner or polish to the instrument that is not designed specifically for string instruments.

■ *Cracks.* A crack in a string instrument should not be taken lightly. Some cracks are not reparable. Whether or not the crack can and should be repaired depends on several things: the size of the crack, the location of the crack, if the repair to the crack will hold and if the cost of the repair exceeds the value of the instrument. Only a qualified string repair person will be able to answer these questions. This is a good time to take steps to prevent future accidents (see maintenance and storage section above).

- *Solutions:* Take the instrument to a qualified string repair shop. Replace the instrument if it cannot be repaired.

■ *Buzzing or Rattling Sound*

■ Buzzing or rattling sounds can have many causes. The seven most likely causes are listed below:

- *Fine Tuners.* Nothing should be loose, especially the circular screw or nut on top. In addition, no part of the metal should be contacting the wood underneath.

- *Chin rest.* No part of the metal should be loose. For tightening instructions, see Chapter 2: Troubleshooting: Chin Rest.

- *Strings.* Check for unraveling and any string cutting into the bridge. Any string where the metal is unraveling from extended use should be replaced. No string should be cutting deeply into the bridge or into the nut at the end of the fingerboard causing a pinched sound (see maintenance section: bridge above).

- *Open Seams.* There should be no openings in the seams that join the back of the instrument to the center or along the edges joining the front to the sides. Check the entire edge along both sides of the upper bout, lower bout and c bout. To detect open seams that cannot be seen, simply knock gently on the edges with a knuckle and listen for any place that changes sound. This repair should only be done by a qualified repairman.

- *Fingerboard.* The fingerboard should look fairly even without excessive denting in it. For solutions, see "Fingerboard Loose or Excessive Denting."

- *Shoulder pad.* For violin and viola, only the rubber feet of the shoulder pad should be contacting the wood on the back of the instrument, no other part including the long center part should touch. To correct this, heighten the feet of the shoulder pad by turning the screws that are adjustable.

- *Mute.* This will buzz or rattle if not properly secured on the string.

■ *Fingerboard Loose or Dented*

- ■ *Loose.* The fingerboard may become loose if the environment is too humid because of excessive heat. Strive to keep the instrument at room temperature.

  - *Solution:* Take the instrument to a qualified string repair shop to have the fingerboard re-glued.

- ■ *Dented.* Over time, dents can form in the fingerboard as the fingers are repeatedly pressed down. You might hear a rattling sound when the string comes in contact with the fingerboard or you may be finding accurate intonation very difficult, especially on double-stops or shifting.

  - *Solutions:* 1. Take the instrument to a qualified string repair shop to have the fingerboard planed. 2. Strive to maintain consistent temperature and humidity control (see Temperature and Moisture Control above)

▮ *Instrument Sliding Away or Issues with Endpins*

- For Violin/Viola, see Chapter 2: Accessories

- For Cello, see Chapter 3: Troubleshooting and Repair

- For Bass, see Chapter 4: Troubleshooting and Repair

Tool Kit

Head off problems by creating a *String Instrument Repair Kit* to keep the following items handy:

- Pliers (repairs stuck endpins, fine tuners, or bass bridges)

- Extra Set of Strings for Each Instrument (repairs broken strings)

- Chin Rest Tightener or Large Paper Clip (repairs loose, rattling or falling off chin rests)

- Extra Rosin for Each Instrument (repairs uneven sound)

- Extra Rockstop (repairs slipping cellos or basses)

- Rubbing Alcohol (removes rosin and dirt from fingerboard and strings)

- Kohlstein Instrument Cleaner and Polish (removes excessive rosin build-up and dirt)

- Soft, Dry, Lint-free Cleaning Cloths (removes rosin, dirt, and fingerprints)

- Dampit In-Instrument Humidifier (repairs problems related to moisture control)

VIOLIN AND VIOLA

Purchasing

■ *Recommended Student Instruments*

Below is a list of student model instruments of the minimum quality and durability acceptable to many school districts across the country. They are listed alphabetically, not in order of preference. They can be found at local area music stores in most places.

VIOLIN	VIOLA
Eastman 80 or 100	Geller 201
Erik Wagner 120 or 131	Glaesel VA10
Geller 120P	Joseph Geisler
Glaesel VI31	Knilling 3104
Joseph Geisler	Otto Benjamin
Knilling 10K (or 8K)	Otto Klier
Otto Benjamin	Scherl & Roth 403
Otto Klier	Strobel MA85
Scherl & Roth 301	Wagner 201 or 203
Strobel ML85	Franz Hoffman
Franz Hoffman	Klaus Mueller
Klaus Mueller	Eastman

Instruments to Avoid

■ Any instrument that is not the natural wood color (black, white, pink, blue, etc.). Painted instruments do not vibrate in the same way that varnished instruments do and will not produce a characteristic tone.

■ Many teachers report repeated problems with the following brands: Cecilio, Mendini, Cremona, Cresent, Palatino, Lark, Skylark and First

Act. In addition, many teachers have noted significant problems with Chinese instruments not made of real wood or ebony parts and with inexpensive instruments purchased on EBay that cannot be tried out, approved by a teacher, or returned easily. For this reason, many teachers recommend against purchasing any string instrument you have not first played on. Many of these poor quality instruments cost more to have set-up properly (bridge, fingerboard, strings, sound post) than the instrument itself may be worth. This can cost $200 or more just to make the violin or viola functional.

Renting vs. Buying Student Model Instruments

- Beginning violin and viola students should rent instruments from a local reputable dealer rather than buy instruments, especially if they are not starting on a full size. Dr. Jacob Dakon of the University of Kansas offers these reasons for renting over buying with which I totally agree:

  - If a student begins on a smaller ½ or ¾ size instrument, the rental dealer will usually buy back the smaller instrument and provide the students with a proper size at little to no additional cost. Smaller sized instruments are typically difficult to sell.

  - If a student quits, the monetary investment has been small and the instrument is returned to the dealer.

  - Students have accidents and rental instruments are typically under a dealer warranty.

Step-up and Professional Instruments

- Good quality step-up and professional instruments tend to be hand-made and varnished by an individual maker or workshop, not machine-made with pre-assembled parts. They are made of higher quality wood, ebony parts, and show greater attention to detail and workmanship. At this level, the "tiger striping" or "highly flamed" effect on the varnish is usually present rather than a shiny, mono-colored finish. Although this effect is decorative and doesn't impact the quality of the sound, it is almost always found on higher quality instruments.

- Step-up quality instruments should be purchased from a reputable luthier, violin shop, or reputable online company. Most violin shops sell all four string instruments, not just violins. An intermediate violin can cost between $2,000 and $5,000. Advanced violins can range from $5,000 to millions of dollars. Violas share this wide range, but are slightly higher in price due to the larger size of the instrument.

- Step up recommendations: Eastman Torelli Sonata, Franz Hoffman Etude (a step up from the Franz Hoffman prelude), and Rudolph Doetsch instruments.

- Professional quality instruments should be purchased based on the quality of the sound, ease of action (playability), and quality of the workmanship, not on brand or label (as these are often falsified). Of course, a verifiable Guarneri, Stradivarius or Amati is worth its weight in gold and are well beyond the price range of most performing professional musicians. They are played mostly by the world's leading soloists or kept in museums or private collections. Beware- there are a multitude of "Stradivarius" instruments on the market that are not authentic.

■ *Bows*

- Student model instruments generally come with durable fiberglass bows (not real wood and not real horse hair).

- Step-up instruments should include a better quality bow made of real wood (Pernambuco or Brazilwood) or high quality carbon fiber and should not contain plastic pieces in the frog or tip.

- Professional instruments and bows are generally purchased separately, but should be well matched for sound. The most popular woods are Pernambuco and Brazilwood and these bows should contain ebony frog, ivory tip, and high quality metal for the ferrule.

Accessories/Essential Equipment

■ *Shoulder pads (also called shoulder rests)*

- Recommended: Kun Collapsible or Wolf

- Other Acceptable Brands: Knilling VIVA, Everest

- Avoid: sponges. They tend to slide and are not adjustable to individual neck size.

■ *Strings*

- Recommended: Thomastic Dominant

- Other Acceptable Brands: D'Addario Helicore, Chromcore, Piranito or Prelude strings.

- Avoid: steel strings (Super-Sensitive). They produce a very bright, harsh sound and wear out easily.

■ *Rosin*

- Student: D'Addario Natural Rosin

- Step-Up: Pirastro Goldflex, Hidersine, or Hill

- Avoid: Super Sensitive. It creates a harsh tone.

- Warning: never use bass or cello rosin on a violin or viola bow. They are much stickier and tend to clump and damage the bow hair.

■ *Soft Cloth*

- Only use soft materials to wipe off fingerprints and rosin from the instrument after each use. Any soft cloth made of the following materials will work: 1.cotton (such as the kind found in old t-shirts), 2. microfiber (found in dedicated instrument wiping cloths). Avoid any harsh materials like those in wash cloths, towels or socks. These scratch the finish.

■ *Mute*

- Performance mutes are lightweight, usually made of rubber, and alter the character of the sound, making it softer and darker. Tourte is the most popular brand, but any on the market are acceptable.

- Practice mutes are heavier, dramatically reduce the sound of the instrument, and are generally not used in performance. Any mute made of rubber or metal work well for practice purposes.

Practice Mutes   Performance Mutes

Maintenance and Storage

For the following maintenance topics, please see "Strings in General: Problems and Solutions Applicable to All String Instruments"

- Daily Cleaning with Soft Cloth

- Removing Rosin and Fingerprints

- Approved cleaners

- Removal of Accessories for Storage

- Bow Maintenance: Loosening and Preventing Warping, Finger Oils

- Temperature and Moisture Control

Troubleshooting and Repair

■ *Broken Strings*

Students should keep an extra set of strings on hand to replace worn-out, broken or false strings. In replacing strings, it is important to only remove one string at a time so that the bridge does not fall and the alignment of the bridge on the instrument remains constant. This can be easily done by the teacher and there is no need to send the instrument to a music store or repair shop that can leave the student unable to play for several days.

- To replace a string, use these steps:

    1. Remove the old string,

    2. Thread the end of the new string all the way through the hole in the peg until you see it poke through the other side. Do not let it go as you do the next step.

    3. Attach the ball end of the string into the fine-tuner (or through the hole in the tailpiece if you do not have a fine tuner). If the string only has a loop end then hook that to the fine tuner.

    4. Wind the string forward towards the scroll so the string is wrapping over the peg (not under) until the

Remove old string

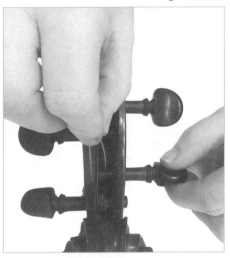
Insert new string through peg hole

Attach ball end into fine tuner

string is tight. Be sure to push the peg inward as you turn and to wind the string towards the peg wall to prevent slipping. This means on violin, G and D strings should be wound towards the left peg wall if the instrument is facing you. E and A should be wound towards the right wall. For viola, C and G wind to the left wall and A and D wind to the right wall. Check the bridge. Be sure the string is in the groove and that the bridge has not moved left or right. The four strings should be centered over the fingerboard. The string should be in the groove at the nut at the end of the fingerboard as well.

■ *Chin Rest Loose or Falling Off*

■ The chin rest on a violin or viola can often become loose and even fall off due to normal wear and tear. If the grooves are not stripped out, you can place the chin rest back on the instrument (being sure to align it correctly over the tailpiece- as pictured below) and re-tighten it. Use either a designated "chin rest tightener" (see below) that can be purchased from most music stores or simply bend a large paper clip to serve as the tool (see below). As you look down onto the top of the instrument, turn the tool counterclockwise until you feel the screw tighten and fit snuggly. Do not overtighten or you will strip the grooves. If you use a paperclip, keep an eye on the wood of the instrument to be sure you do not scratch it by poking the paperclip all the way through.

■ The chin rest can be replaced if it is stripped. Consider the Stuber Ebony Violin or Viola Chin rest- Medium Plate from Shar Music for student model instruments.

Chin rest tightener

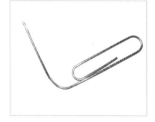

Paper clip as tool

■ *Broken or Malfunctioning Fine Tuner*

■ It is important for beginning students to have four well-functioning fine tuners on their instrument to facilitate ease of tuning and to prevent broken strings caused by turning pegs. There are two types (see below). The ball end is most common for student instruments and should be used with all strings that have a ball end. The loop end fine tuner is most often used only for the highest string (E string on violin or A string on the viola), but can work for any strings that do not have a ball end.

- Although is is possible to hook a loop end string onto a ball end tuner, it is not advised because the sharp edges and friction tend to break the string. Most professional instruments have no fine tuners except for the one for the highest string (loop end).

Ball end   Loop end

- If the fine tuner is not working, first check that it is not overly tightened and digging into the wood beneath. This should be corrected immediately by loosening the tuner and tightening the peg. Students should be warned not to overtighten the tuner (see below).

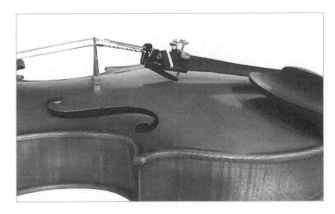

Do not let fine tuner scratch wood!

- Screws that are difficult to turn can be lubricated by unscrewing them and either spraying WD-40 on the grooves or lubricating the grooves with Ivory bar soap. If the screw cannot be repaired, it can be replaced with a Violin or Viola 2 Prong String Adjuster Post-Type.

Be sure to order the appropriate size for the instrument (for example, 4/4, 3/4, 2/4).

- To install a fine tuner follow these steps:

  1. Remove the old fine tuner by completely unscrewing the screw and removing the base.

  2. Thread the new fine tuner base up through the opening on the tailpiece.

  3. Tighten the circular mounting screw onto the base.

  4. Tighten the tuning screw into the base through the circular mounting screw and place the string into the new fine tuner as shown below.

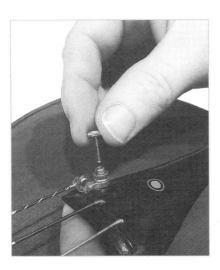

Buzzing Sound

Check the following:

- *Fine tuner screws.* Nothing should be loose, especially the circular mounting screw on top.

- *Underneath the fine tuner.* No part of the metal should be contacting the wood.

- *Unraveling strings.* Any string where the metal is unraveling from extended use should be replaced.

- *Open Seams.* There should be no openings in the seams that join the back of the instrument to the center or along the edges joining the front to the sides. Check the entire edge along both sides of the upper bout, lower bout and c bout. This repair should be done by a qualified string instrument repairman.

- *Strings.* No string should be cutting deeply into the bridge or into the nut at the end of the fingerboard causing a pinched sound.

- *Shoulder Pad.* Only the rubber feet of the shoulder pad should be contacting the wood on the back, no other part including the long center part should touch. To correct this, heighten the feet of the shoulder pad by turning the screws that are adjustable.

- *Mute.* This will buzz or rattle if not properly secured.

For the following topics, please see "Strings in General: Problems and Solutions Applicable to All String Instruments: Troubleshooting and Repair:"

- Pegs Slipping or Sticking

- Bow Will Not Tighten

- Bow Will Not Loosen

- Bow Hairs Broken

- Bow Makes No Sound

- Bow Will Not Produce a Consistent Tone

- Bridge Broken or Cracked

- Fallen Bridge

- Bridge is Leaning or Bumped Out of Position

- Sound Post Down

- Scratches or Cracks in Wood

- Fingerboard Loose or Dented

CELLO

Purchasing

■ *Recommended Student Instruments*

Below is a list of student model instruments of minimum quality and durability acceptable to many school districts across the country. They are listed alphabetically, not in order of preference. They can be found at local area music stores in most places. I highly recommend that beginning students rent rather than buy instruments, especially if they are not playing a full size instrument as these are not easily resold and generally don't hold their value.

Glaesel—Model CE42 or CE44
Hermann Beyer
Knilling Bucharest 157F or 152F
Otto Benjamin
Scherl & Roth 503 or RC97E4 (advanced)
Eastman VC80, VC90, VC95, VC100
Franz Hoffman
Klaus Mueller

Instruments to Avoid

- ■ Painted vs. Varnished Instruments
    - • Any instrument that is not the natural wood color (black, white, pink, blue, etc.) since painted instruments do not vibrate in the same way that varnished instruments do and generally will not produce a characteristic tone.

- ■ Problematic Brands

  - ● Many teachers report repeated problems with the following brands: Cecilio, Mendini, Cremona, Cresent, Palatino, Lark, Skylark and First Act.

  - ● Teachers in school districts that have purchased Engelhardt cellos report persistent problems with the following: pegs that strip (won't stay in place), bridges and sound posts that fall easily, fingerboards that may be a bit askew making proper bridge placement and string alignment difficult, endpins that need to be replaced because they are too short to fit most students, and necks that may be a bit thicker than other brands (making fingering accuracy more challenging). There are some teachers who report no such issues.

- ■ Instruments that Cannot be Tried Out and Approved by a Teacher First

  - ● Multiple teachers have noted significant problems with Chinese instruments not made of real wood or ebony parts and with other inexpensive instruments purchased on EBay or other websites that cannot be tried out, approved by a teacher, or returned easily. For this reason, many teachers recommend against purchasing any string instrument you have not first played. Many of these poor quality instruments cost more to have set-up properly (bridge, fingerboard, strings, sound post) than the instrument itself is worth.

- ■ Renting vs. Buying Student Model Instruments

  - ● Beginning cello students should rent instruments from a local reputable dealer rather than buy instruments, especially if they are not starting on a full size. Dr. Jacob Dakon of the University of Kansas offers these reasons for renting over buying:

    - » If a student begins on a smaller ½ or ¾ size instrument, the rental dealer will usually buy back the smaller instrument and provide the student with a proper size at little to no additional cost. Smaller size instruments are typically difficult to sell.

    - » If a student quits, the monetary investment has been small and the instrument is returned to the dealer.

    - » Students have accidents and rental instruments are typically under a dealer warranty.

■ *Step-up and Professional Instruments*

- ■ Good quality step-up and professional cellos tend to be hand-carved by an individual from spruce or maple, rather than being machine-made from plywood laminate with preassembled parts. As with the violin and viola, the workmanship shows a greater attention to detail at this level. The "tiger striping" or "highly flamed" effect on the varnish is usually present rather than a shiny, mono-colored finish. Although this effect is decorative and doesn't impact the quality of the sound, it is almost always found on higher quality instruments.

- Step-up quality instruments should be purchased from a reputable luthier, violin shop or reputable online company. Most violin shops sell all four string instruments, not just violins.

- Professional quality instruments should be purchased based on the quality of the sound, ease of action (playability), and quality of the workmanship, not on brand or label (as these can be falsified).

■ *Bows*

- Student model instruments generally come with durable fiberglass bows (not real wood and not real horse hair).

- Step-up instruments should include a better quality bow made of real wood (Pernambuco or Brazilwood) or high quality carbon fiber and should not contain plastic pieces in the frog or tip.

- Professional instruments and bows are generally purchased separately, but should be well-matched for sound. The most popular woods are Pernambuco and Brazilwood and these bows should contain ebony frog, ivory tip, and high quality metal for the ferrule.

Accessories/Essential Equipment

■ *Rockstops or Straps*

- All cellists need either a freestanding rockstop or a strap that connects to the chair to prevent the cello from sliding while playing (unless they have had the endpin professionally sharpened—not recommended for students for safety reasons!). Although, some cellos may come with a rubber endpin tip cover, these generally do not work as well on all surfaces to keep the instrument from slipping while playing.

  - Recommended Rockstop Brands: Rockstop Endpin Rest, Dycem Black Hole Endpin Stop

  - Recommended Strap: Xeros Endpin Anchor strap

  - Other Acceptable Brands: Glaesel

- Note: In an emergency situation, it is possible (though, not ideal) for performers to use a shoe to place the endpin in or place a car mat underneath the leg of the chair and endpin. There are also a variety of other creative solutions that can be found by wedging non-slip materials against the music stand.

Rockstop

Strap/Endpin Anchor

Endpin Tip Cover

■ *Strings*

- ■ Recommended Brands: Larsen, D'Addario Helicore, Jargar

- ■ Other Acceptable Brands: Pirastro Chromcore, Corelli, Thomastik Dominant or Spirocore, Prim, D'Addario Prelude

- ■ Avoid: steel strings (Super-Sensitive). They produce a very bright, harsh sound and wear out easily.

■ *Rosin*

- ■ Several things should be considered when selecting a rosin that can bring out the best tone quality of a particular cello including the type of strings on the instrument and the climate. Generally, softer rosins tend to work better if the cello is equipped with synthetic or gut strings whereas darker rosins tend to work better with steel strings or those with other types of metal in the core. Trying out several different rosins will allow each individual to select the best rosin for bringing out the tone they prefer.

  - ● Recommended Student Brands: D'Addario Natural Rosin

  - ● Recommended Step-Up Brands: Kaplan, Goldflex, Hidersine, Hill

  - ● Avoid: Super Sensitive. It creates a harsh tone.

    - » ***Warning:*** Avoid using bass rosin on a cello bow. Bass rosin is softer and stickier than violin, viola or cello rosin and is designed for different amounts of friction on larger strings.

■ *Soft Cloth*

- ■ Only use soft materials to wipe off fingerprints and rosin from the instrument after each use. Any soft cloth made of the following materials will work: 1.cotton (such as the kind found in old t-shirts), 2. microfiber (found in dedicated instrument wiping cloths). Avoid any harsh materials like those in wash cloths, towels or socks. These scratch the finish.

■ *Mute*

- ■ Performance mutes are lightweight, usually made of rubber, and alter the character of the sound, making it softer and darker. Tourte is the most popular brand, but any on the market are acceptable.

- ■ Practice mutes are heavier, dramatically reduce the sound of the instrument, and are generally not used in performance. Any mute made of rubber or metal work well for practice purposes.

Maintenance and Storage

- ■ Maintenance and Care:
  - ● Place the cello on its side with the endpin in when not being played. Never lay the cello on its back because this places too much stress on the neck and heel joint.
  - ● The bow should be placed on the music stand or a flat surface when not being played. Never place the bow on the floor (where it can get dirty or stepped on) or a chair (where it can likely be sat on).
  - ● For the following maintenance topics, please see "Strings in General: Problems and Solutions Applicable to All String Instruments"
    - » Daily Cleaning with Soft Cloth
    - » Removing Rosin and Fingerprints
    - » Approved cleaners
    - » Removal of Accessories for Storage
    - » Bow Maintenance
      - ◆ Loosening and Preventing Warping
      - ◆ Finger Oils
    - » Temperature Control
    - » Humidity and Moisture Control

- Storage:
  - Cases (2 types):
    - » Soft Cases
      - ◆ Soft cases are most often provided with beginner instruments. It is important to insert the cello face up, with bridge and bow pocket aligned in order to avoid undue stress on the bridge. Nylon cases with no padding should be avoided as these provide little protection for the instrument and bow.
    - » Hard Cases
      - ◆ Although hard cases are more expensive than soft cases, cellists with high quality step-up or professional instruments (or musicians who travel frequently) often prefer a hard case because it provides much greater protection for these fragile, hand-made instruments.
  - Endpins
    - » Cellos should always be stored with the endpin in and the screw left in the tightened position in order to prevent the following problems:
      - ◆ the endpin from falling out
      - ◆ wear and tear on the endpin housing that can cause it to strip
      - ◆ damage to the wood and/or endpin housing of the cello caused by the endpin hitting other objects during the process of placing it in a storage rack or case.
  - Bows
    - » Cello bows should be stored with the bow hair in the loosened position in order to prevent warping of the bow stick caused by prolonged tension.
    - » When storing a bow in a soft cello case, it is important to put the bow in the case after the cello is in place and has been zipped in securely. Placing the bow in the case before the cello increases the likelihood that the bow stick or tip may become broken in the storage process. When unpacking a cello from a soft case, it is important to remove the bow first (before the cello) for the same reason.
    - » When storing a bow in a hard cello case, it is important to be sure the plastic storage handle is securely in the closed position that immobilizes the bow; otherwise, the bow will fall out of the holder and scratch the surface of the cello.

Troubleshooting and Repair

■ *Endpin Stuck in Place (won't pull out or push in)*

- ▣ Check to see if the endpin is bent.

- ▣ If not bent:
  - ● Twist the endpin back and forth as you pull it out or push in. Be sure that the endpin screw is loosened while doing this.
  - ● If this does not work, take the endpin all the way out and spray a lubricating agent like WD-40 on a cloth and then wipe the entire surface of the endpin with it before reinserting it.

- ▣ If bent:
  - ● Remove it and replace it with a new one. These can be purchased online or through your local music store. This is a simple repair and most teachers are capable of replacing this without sending the instrument to a repair shop as the new endpin should slide easily into the place left by the old one.

■ *Endpin Stuck Inside of the Cello*

- ▣ Check to see if it will come out of one of the *f* holes (usually will not work unless the opening is wide, but worth a try).

- ▣ Use an auto tool called a "claw grabber pick-up tool" that has a retractable grabbing end to pull it out.

- ▣ If you feel comfortable doing so, remove the endpin housing carefully after loosening strings (see diagram below) and then use a wire hanger to pull it out. If you do not feel comfortable doing this, a local repairman can remove the endpin from the instrument. Be careful of the bridge so it doesn't break and take care not to knock over the sound post on the inside. A qualified repairman is always the safest option.

■ *Endpin Slips Down (won't stay in place)*

- ▣ Check the Screw:
  - ● If it is loose, tighten it securely. Be careful not to over-tighten or the screw will strip out and no longer be usable. Students should be made aware of this as well as the importance of not pushing the endpin in with the screw tight. Students should never lean their body weight onto a tightened endpin. This causes stripping.

- If the screw is not properly aligned with the grooves of the opening, realign it and screw it back in.

- If the grooves on the screw are stripped out, replace it.

■ Check the Housing:

- If it is stripped or coming away from the instrument, send it to a qualified string repair shop.

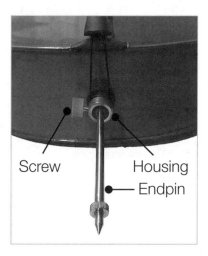

Screw   Housing
            — Endpin

■ For the following repair topics, please see "Strings in General: Problems and Solutions Applicable to All String Instruments: Troubleshooting and Repair:"

- Pegs Slipping or Sticking

- Bow Will Not Tighten

- Bow Will Not Loosen

- Bow Hairs Broken

- Bow Makes No Sound

- Bow Will Not Produce a Consistent Tone

- Bridge Broken or Cracked

- Fallen Bridge

- Bridge is Leaning or Bumped Out of Position

- Sound Post Down

- Scratches or Cracks in Wood

- Fingerboard Loose or Dented

- Cracks in Instrument

■ For information on broken strings or malfunctioning fine tuners, please see "Violin and Viola: Troubleshooting and Repair."

BASS

Purchasing

■ *Recommended Student Instruments*

■ Below is a list of student model instruments acceptable to many school districts across the country. They are listed alphabetically, not in order of preference. I highly recommend that beginning students rent rather than buy instruments, especially if they are not playing a ¾ bass. Smaller instruments are not as easily resold and generally don't hold their value.

Christopher
Eastman
Glaesel –DB66
Knilling Bucharest 1302T, 1308T
Franz Hoffman
Klaus Mueller
Shen

■ The most common size basses found in schools are: ¼, ½, and ¾. Students should never play a bass that is too large for them or they risk physical injury (see Chapter 1: "Instrument Selection and Sizing" for details). It is very rare for anyone (even adult professionals) to play a 4/4 bass. These are rarely made or sold because the distance between even the smallest interval exceeds the average distance of what the human hand/fingers can reach without shifting.

■ For younger students (and for all school settings), it is best to look for an instrument that balances durability with tone. Instruments that produce the best tone tend to be the least durable. This means they can be easily damaged by students, and may need frequent, costly repairs.

■ Step-up Instruments

■ Whereas beginner quality basses are usually laminate/plywood throughout, step-up quality basses should be either a mixture of laminate and real wood (usually a carved spruce top with laminate back and sides) or contain no laminate. Both "Hybrid" and fully carved wood basses produce a richer tone. They are, however, much more delicate and damage more easily. They are most often found in high school programs and played by more advanced students.

■ Step-up quality instruments should be purchased based on the quality of the sound, ease of action (playability), and quality of the set-up and workmanship, not on brand or label (as these can be falsified).

■ Professional Instruments

■ Professional quality basses are fully hand-carved by an individual maker (not machine-made). They feature high quality wood like spruce or maple. The "tiger striping" or a "highly flamed" effect on the varnish is almost always present rather than a shiny, mono-colored finish found on laminate or most hybrid basses. Although this effect is decorative and doesn't impact the quality of the sound, it is almost always found on higher quality instruments.

■ Professional quality instruments should be purchased based on the quality of the sound, ease of action (playability), and quality of the set-up and workmanship, not on brand or label (as these can be falsified). These instruments should be purchased from a reputable luthier/violin shop. Most violin shops sell all four string instruments, not just violins.

Instruments to Avoid

■ Instruments not Set-Up by a Qualified String Repair Person

● ***Quality of the set-up*** is one of the most important things to consider when purchasing a bass because this greatly impacts both playability and tone. Be sure to inquire if the bridge, nut and sound post have been set-up by an actual repair person before purchase (not just using pre-assembled parts cut by machine). Even a good quality bass will not play well or sound good if it is not set-up properly. For this reason, many bass players consider the quality of the set-up (especially on a beginner bass) equally if not more important than the brand name.

■ Instruments that are Painted Colors Instead of Varnished

● Avoid any instrument that is not the natural wood color. Painted instruments do not vibrate in the same way that varnished instruments do and generally will not produce a characteristic tone.

- Instruments that Cannot be Tried Out First or Returned without Penalty

  - Multiple teachers have noted significant problems with Chinese instruments not made of real wood or ebony parts and with other inexpensive instruments purchased online on EBay or other websites that cannot be tried out, approved by a teacher, or returned easily. For this reason, many teachers recommend against purchasing any string instrument you have not first played. Many of these poor quality instruments cost more to have set-up properly (bridge, fingerboard, strings, sound post) than the instrument itself is worth.

- Problematic Brands:

  - Many teachers report repeated problems with the following brands: Cecilio, Mendini, Cremona, Cresent, Palatino, Lark, Skylark and First Act.

Renting vs. Buying Student Model Instruments

- Beginning bass students should rent instruments from a local reputable dealer rather than buy instruments, especially if they are not starting on a ¾ size. String specialist, Dr. Jacob Dakon of the University of Kansas offers these compelling reasons for renting over buying:

  - If a student begins on a smaller instrument, the rental dealer will usually buy back the smaller instrument and provide the student with a proper size at little to no additional cost. Smaller size instruments are typically difficult to sell.

  - If a student quits, the monetary investment has been small and the instrument is returned to the dealer.

  - Students have accidents and rental instruments are typically under a dealer warranty.

■ *Bows*

- Two Types

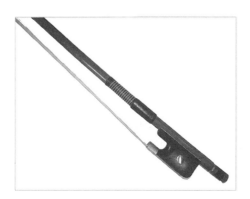 

French Bow   German Bow

- ■ Bow Selection
  - ● Both French and German bows are equally acceptable. Selection generally comes down to personal preference and pedagogical considerations. You will find professionals equally committed to either type of bow.
  - ● Many schools purchase a class set of French Bows, but also keep one or two German Bows on hand for those students who prefer them (either because their private instructor taught them this way and they own a German Bow at home, or they are struggling to master the French Bow hold). Reasons for classroom use of French Bow include:
    - » Instructional Ease. The initial bow hold instruction for the French Bow hold is very similar to that for violin, viola and cello. This makes it easier to teach in a heterogeneous class setting
    - » Tension and Success. Young beginners have a tendency to collapse the hand and squeeze when starting with the German bow hold whereas those who switch over to German Bow later with a private instructor tend to do very well.
- ■ Bow Recommendations
  - ● Student
    - » Student model instruments generally come with a durable fiberglass bow such as Glasser.
  - ● Step-Up
    - » Upgrading the bow quality can increase playability and quality of sound. For this purpose, consider a carbon fiber bow or the low end (meaning less expensive) Brazilwood or Pernambuco bows. These bows are generally sold separately from the bass.
  - ● Professional

    The most popular professional quality bows are made from high quality wood (such as Pernambuco or Brazilwood) and should contain an ebony frog, ivory tip, and high quality metal for the ferrule (no plastic pieces). These bows are sold separately from the bass, but should be tried out so that they are well-matched to the specific instrument you intend to play them on. The same bow will sound different on different instruments.

Accessories/Essential Equipment

■ *Rockstop or Strap*

- All bassists need either a freestanding rockstop or a strap that connects to the stool in order to prevent the bass from sliding. Although, some basses may come with a rubber endpin tip cover, these generally do not work as well on all surfaces.

  - Recommended Rockstop: Rockstop Bass Endpin Rest, Dycem Black Hole Endpin Stop

  - Recommended Strap: Xeros Endpin Anchor Strap

  - Emergency: In an emergency situation, it is possible (though, not ideal) for performers to use a shoe to place their endpin in or to place a car mat, carpet square or other material underneath the leg of the stool and endpin. There are also a variety of other creative solutions that can be found by wedging non-slip materials against the music stand or under the stool.

Rockstop   Strap/Endpin Anchor   Endpin Tip Cover

■ *Strings*

- Good quality strings are essential to produce a characteristic tone. *Bass strings almost never break*, but tend to lose their ability to draw a consistent pitch, becoming "false." For this reason, try to replace the strings every 1–3 years as financially feasible. For school programs on a limited budget, basses can be placed on a rotation so that each year one set is replaced. It is impossible for an orchestra to sound in tune if the bass strings are not producing a consistent pitch.

  - Recommended Brand: D'Addario Helicore (medium gauge) or Thomastik Spirocore for Jazz

  - Other Acceptable Brands: D'Addario Prelude

- Step-Up Quality: Kaplan, Bel Canto, Corelli
- Avoid: Steel strings (Super-Sensitive). They produce a very bright, harsh sound and wear out easily.

■ *Rosin*

- ■ High quality rosin is crucial for gripping the large strings and producing a good tone on the bass. This is more crucial for bass than of any other string instrument (due the string size and amount of friction needed). The importance of a good quality rosin for bass players cannot be overstated. Recommendations are below:
  - Recommended Brands: Pops
  - Other Acceptable Brands: Kolstein (soft), Carlsson, Nyman
  - Avoid: Super Sensitive. It creates a harsh, bright tone on most basses.
    - » ***Warning:*** Rosin should be applied to the bass bow ***only in the downward motion*** (traveling from frog to tip). Traveling in both directions can damage bow hairs, causing them to rip out of the bow. Bass rosin only works if it still retains its moisture (not dried out). For common rosin-related issues and solutions such as those listed below, see "Troubleshooting and Repair" later in this chapter:
  - Rosin Clumped on Bow Hair
  - Rosin No Longer Works
  - Rosin Hard to Get Out or Stuck to Wrapper

■ *Soft Cloth*

- ■ Only use soft materials to wipe off fingerprints and rosin from the instrument after each use. Any soft cloth made of the following materials will work: 1.cotton (such as the kind found in old t-shirts), 2. microfiber (found in dedicated instrument wiping cloths). Avoid any harsh materials like those in wash cloths, towels or socks. These scratch the finish.

■ *Mute*

- ■ Performance mutes are lightweight, usually made of rubber, and alter the character of the sound, making it softer and darker. Tourte is the most popular brand, but any on the market are acceptable.
- ■ Practice mutes are heavier, dramatically reduce the sound of the instrument, and are generally not used in performance. Any heavy-duty mute will work well for practice purposes.

■ Stools (Optional)

■ There are two acceptable ways to position a bass while playing: 1. Standing position (requires no stool), and 2. Sitting position (requires a stool). Both sitting and standing positions are acceptable and used widely among professional players and in schools. If student bass players sit, the stool at home and at school must be matched precisely to their height. Many teachers prefer to start all beginning bass players standing (for the logistical and pedagogical reasons listed below) and then later allow choices based on individual preference, private teacher request, and/or differentiation needs. Below are common stool uses and considerations with each type of positioning.

- Standing Position/ Stool as Rest

  » If the "standing position" is used, no stool is needed. Many schools, do however, still provide stools for students to rest on during rehearsal as this can prevent students (with training) from leaning their full body weight on the instrument and stripping out the endpin. The endpin is not designed to hold body weight.

  » It is difficult to provide a perfectly matched height of stool for each student in each class both at home and in the classroom. Being inconsistent with the height of stool is detrimental to students' ability to achieve a consistently correct playing position.

- Sitting Position on a Stool

  » If a student sits on a stool to play, it is crucial that the stool used for home practice and classroom rehearsal be the exact same type and height in order to promote proper body balance and consistent instrument set-up/holding technique.

  » **Warning:** If the stool is too high and the body is off balance, accidents can occur causing physical injury to the student and damage to the instrument.

  » Sizing: The stool is the proper height if the top of the stool contacts the student at the intersection of the top of the leg and the bottom of the buttock. Students will need to be trained to adjust stool height each class period if stools are shared in the school setting and to reset their stool height whenever they have a growth spurt.

Maintenance and Storage

Maintenance:

- Instrument:

  - Use a soft cloth to wipe fingerprints and rosin off of the bass after every use.

  - Never lean your body weight onto the instrument or attempt to push the endpin in without loosening the screw. This will strip out the endpin and it will have to be replaced.

  - When not being played and not in the case, place the bass on its side with the endpin in. Never lay the bass on its back because this places too much stress on the neck and heel joint.

- Bow

  - Never touch the bow hair with your fingers. It will be damaged by the oil and no longer hold rosin.

  - Always tighten the bow before use and loosen it after use in order to prevent the stick from warping.

  - When not being played and not in the case, place the bow on the music stand, or on a flat surface. Never place the bow on the floor (where it can get dirty or stepped on) or on a chair.

- For the following maintenance topics, please see "Strings in General: Problems and Solutions Applicable to All String Instruments"

  - Temperature Control

  - Humidity and Moisture Control

Storage:

- Cases (2 types): Soft and Hard

  - Soft Cases

    » Soft cases with padding are most common. When storing the bass, be sure to insert it face up (with the bridge side of the instrument touching the bow side of the case) in order to avoid undue stress on the bridge. Nylon cases with no padding should be avoided as these provide little protection for the instrument and bow.

  - Hard Cases

    » Hard cases are rarely used for regular local transport due to expense, size, and carrying difficulty. They are primarily used by professionals for air travel and are usually cost-prohibitive for students.

- Endpins
  - Basses should always be stored with the endpin in and the screw in the tightened position. The endpin screw must be loosened prior to moving the endpin in any direction and then tightened again once in place. Proper use and storage of the endpin will prevent the following problems:
    - » the endpin from falling out
    - » wear and tear on the endpin housing that can cause it to strip
    - » damage to the wood and/ or endpin housing of the bass caused by the endpin hitting other objects during the process of placing it in a storage rack or case.
- Bows
  - When storing a bow, put the bow in the case after the bass is in place and has been zipped securely in order to avoid breaking the stick or damaging the hair. When unpacking the bass, remove the bow first (before the instrument) for the same reason.
  - Bass bows should be stored in the case with the bow hair in the loosened position. This prevents the stick from warping.
  - While carrying the bass without the case; the bow can be placed beneath the A and E strings with the tip towards the bridge (shown at right) or placed in a bow bag.
    - » *Warning:* Avoid transporting the bow in the F holes. This causes damage to both the wood of the bow and the bass and damages bow hairs.

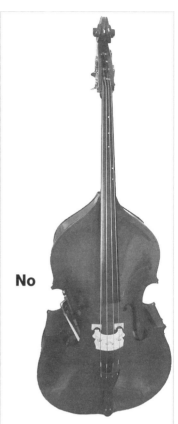

No

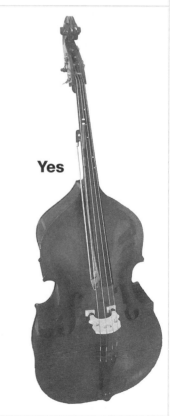

Yes

Troubleshooting and Repair

■ *Strings*

- ■ Too Low (Buzzing) or Too High (Hard to Press Down)

  - ● String are too low if the distance between the fingerboard and strings is so small that strings are difficult to play pizzicato or the string makes a buzzing sound when played.

  - ● String are too high if the distance between the fingerboard and strings is so large that strings are almost impossible to push down and are excessively painful to fingertips.

  - ● To change the string height, turn the adjusters on the bridge with your fingers or with pliers (see below).

  - ● If this does not work, send the instrument to a qualified repair person as they will likely need to adjust the nut height or bridge or both.

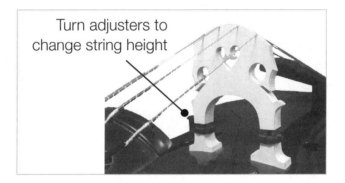

Turn adjusters to change string height

- ■ False (Pitch Wavers)

  - ● String are *false* if the pitch wavers and does not ring true after the bow leaves the string. Bass strings tend to go false long before they break. Professional bassists often replace strings yearly. It is important to get into a regular rotation of replacing the strings on each bass you own at least every few years as financially feasible.

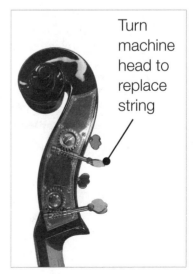

Turn machine head to replace string

- ■ Need to be Replaced (Broken, False, or Fraying)

  - ● For directions on how to replace a string, see "Violin and Viola: Troubleshooting and Repair." Use the same procedure for threading strings through the machine heads (see diagram below) as violin pages.

- Replacing bass strings can be time consuming and painful to arm muscles due to the length of strings and functioning of the tuning mechanism. Some bass players use a "Turbotune Peg Winder" attached to the end of a drill to remedy these issues.

■ *Endpin*

- Stuck in Place (won't pull out or push in)
  - Check to see if the endpin is bent.
    - » If not bent:
      - ◆ Twist the endpin back and forth as you pull it out or push in. Pliers may be needed. Be sure the endpin screw is loosened while doing this.
      - ◆ If this does not work, take the endpin all the way out and spray a lubricating agent like WD-40 on a cloth and then wipe the entire surface of the endpin with it before reinserting it.
    - » If bent:
      - ◆ Remove it and replace it with a new one. These can be purchased online or through your local music store. This is a simple repair and most teachers are capable of replacing this without sending the instrument to a repair shop as the new endpin should slide easily into the place left by the old one.

- Stuck Inside the Bass
  - Check to see if it will come out of one of the f-holes (usually will not work unless the opening is wide, but worth a try).
  - Use a tool called a "claw grabber pick-up tool" that has a retractable grabbing end to pull it out.
  - If you feel comfortable doing so, remove the endpin housing carefully after loosening strings (see diagram below) and then use a wire hanger to pull it out. If you do not feel comfortable doing this, a local repairman can remove the endpin from the instrument. Be careful of the bridge so it doesn't break and take care not to knock over the sound post on the inside. A qualified repairman is always the safest option.

- Slipping (won't stay in place)
  - Check the screw:
    - » If it is loose, tighten it securely. Be careful not to over-tighten or the screw will strip out and no longer be usable. Never push the endpin in with the screw tight.

- » If the screw is not properly aligned with the grooves of the opening in the housing, realign it and screw it back in.

- » If the grooves on the screw are stripped out, replace it.

- Check the Housing:

  If it is stripped out (screw won't turn) or coming away from the instrument, send it to a qualified string repair shop.

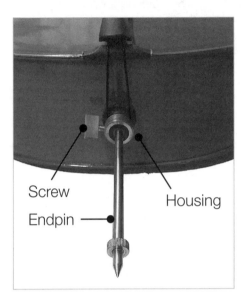

Screw

Endpin

Housing

- ■ Rockstop Sliding Away from Bass

  Rockstops sometimes slip on certain surfaces depending on the material make-up of the floor and its cleanliness. If the rockstop is sliding, place a small amount of saliva on the bottom surface of the rockstop.

■ *Rosin*

- ■ Clumped on the Bow Hair

  - Bass rosin is very sticky and can become clumped on the bow hair if too much is applied. If you see clumps of rosin on the hair, you can comb these out with a regular fine tooth comb found at any department store. Comb the bow in the downward motion (traveling only from the frog to the tip) until clumps are no longer visible and the bow achieves a consistent tone when played.

- ■ No Longer Works (Drying Out)

  - Bass rosin tends to dry out over time and only works well when it is still fresh and contains its moisture. If the rosin is more than a year old, looks dry, or will not come off of the cake even after being scratched with a key, replace it with a fresh new cake.

- Bass rosin will last longer if stored at room temperature. Excessive cold dries it out and excessive heat can melt the rosin into a sticky goo. The rosin should never be left in a hot car or on a heater vent. Do not allow fingers to come in contact with the rosin.

■ Hard to Get Out of Container/Paper Wrapper Stuck to Rosin

To prevent the paper cup wrapping of bass rosin from sticking to the rosin over time (especially, "Pops"), remove the paper wrapping when it is new and store the cake of rosin directly in the plastic cup. Many bass players replace the paper wrapper with a small circular piece of one side of a Ziploc bag which they use to wrap around the rosin, placing both inside of the cup to retain moisture.

For the following repair topics, please see "Strings in General: Problems and Solutions Applicable to All String Instruments: Troubleshooting and Repair:"

- Leaning Bridge

- Cracked Bridge

- Fallen Bridge

- Fallen Sound Post

- Bow Makes No Sound

- Bow not Tightening

- Bow Rehairing

- Bow Hairs Broken

- Fingerboard Loose

- Cracks in Instrument

GLOSSARY

Action   The distance between the string and the fingerboard. If the action is too "high," the strings are too far away from the fingerboard, and are difficult to press down, causing left hand fatigue and reduced playability. If the action is too "low," the string will buzz against the fingerboard.

Adjusting screw   The screw at the frog end of the bow stick which tightens or loosens the hair (clockwise to tighten, counter-clockwise to loosen). Avoid over-tightening the hair while playing, and always remember to loosen the bow hair when finished playing.

Adjustment   The relative placement, height, and angle of all adjustable parts (bridge, sound post, nut, fingerboard, and tailpiece) such that optimal tone and playability are achieved. New instruments require professional set-up performed by a qualified string repair technician before they can be played, and all instruments require occasional maintenance to keep things in proper adjustment.

Amati   A family of string instrument makers from mid-Sixteenth Century Cremona, whose instruments – along with those of Stradivarius and Guarneri – are highly prized for their superlative tone quality.

Ball end string   The type of string that is either threaded through the tailpiece or attached to a two-prong fine tuner. (As opposed to loop end strings, which have no ball, are attached to a one-prong fine tuner, and are most commonly used as the highest string on violins and violas.)

Body   The hollow resonating chamber of a string instrument made up of the top, back and sides (ribs).

Brazilwood   One of the two types of wood used to make high quality bows for string instruments. The other is Pernambuco.

Bridge   The small curved-top piece of maple on the top of the instrument, which transfers string vibrations through the sound post to the body of the instrument. The bridge is held in place by string tension; never apply glue to the bridge.

Bridge height adjusters   Small screw-like metal pieces located on the two feet of a bass bridge, which are used to make minor adjustments to string height as needed due to changes in humidity (not found on violin, violas or cellos).

Bow   The tensioned stick which draws the hair across the string to create vibration and sound.

C Bout   The "waist" or concave indention in the middle of each side of the body (shaped like the letter "C") which allows the highest and lowest strings to be played without the bow contacting the body of the instrument.

Camber   The slight curve downward in the middle of the bow stick (towards the hair). When sighting down the stick from frog to tip, there should be little to no visible curvature left or right.

Carbon fiber bow   A bow stick made of synthetic materials. As they are highly resistant to warping, snapping, and the expansion and contraction caused by temperature and humidity variations, many professionals keep a carbon fiber bow for use at outdoor performances, where a Pernambuco or brazilwood bow would be at risk. High end carbon fiber bow makers offer products designed to rival wooden bows in tone and playability.

Chin rest   On violins and violas, the cupped piece of wood, plastic, or ebony which supports the weight of the player's head while playing. Though called a "chin" rest, it is more accurate to say that the player's mid-jaw is rested here.

Chin rest tightener   A tool used to adjust the metal feet of the chinrest which hold it to the body of the instrument (turn right to tighten, left to loosen). A chin rest should never be over-tightened.

Dampit   A brand name of in-instrument humidifier, consisting of a sponge encased in a rubber sleeve. The Dampit is soaked in water, squeezed dry, and inserted in either the left, right, or both f-holes to help regulate the moisture level of the instrument. Ideal humidity for string instruments is between 30% and 55%.

Denatured alcohol   An ethanol solution which is an ideal solvent for cleaning strings and fingerboards on string instruments. It should never be allowed to come in contact with the body of the instrument, as it will eat away the varnish.

End button   The rounded piece of black wood located at the end of a violin or viola, to which the tailpiece is attached.

Endpin   The retractable spike or rubber tipped metal rod protruding from the bottom of a cello or bass which contacts the floor, allowing the instrument to be positioned at different heights to fit the player. The endpin height is adjusted by tightening and loosening a screw located in the metal collar at the base of the endpin (called the endpin housing).

Endpin strap/anchor   A strap or device that attaches to the leg of a chair (for cellists) or stool (for bassists) to a secure point on the floor in which to seat the endpin and prevent the instrument sliding away while playing.

Eyelet   The threaded metal piece inside the frog of a bow which receives the adjusting screw, allowing the hair to be tightened or loosened.

False String   A string which, due to age or wear-and-tear, is no longer of uniform mass and density along its length, causing it to emit an unstable pitch, or to no longer ring "true" when bowed or plucked.

F-hole   The ornate holes on the top of the body, located to the left and right of the bridge, through which amplified sound waves travel, carrying the final tone from the body of the instrument into the room.

Ferrule   The silver metal tab located at the end of the frog of the bow on a string instrument. It connects the bow hair securely to the frog.

Fine Tuners   The screw-like mechanisms found on the tailpiece of a violin, viola, or cello, which are used to make relatively small adjustments to a string's pitch (turn clockwise to raise the pitch slightly, counter-clockwise to lower the pitch slightly), as opposed to the pegs, located on the scroll, which are capable of much larger pitch adjustments. Student model instruments generally have fine tuners on all four strings, due to their reliability and ease of use for beginning players. Step-up and professional quality instruments generally only use one fine tuner, only on the highest string. Fine tuners are not found on basses.

Fingerboard   The long, smooth, concave black ebony piece on the front of a string instrument that is glued to the neck. The player's fingers push the strings down onto the fingerboard to create different pitches.

Flaming   The striped woodgrain pattern found on the back of higher-quality instruments (as opposed to the shiny, monochromatic finish found on student model instruments). Although the effect is purely decorative, skillfully aligned flaming is often indicative of higher quality workmanship, and is therefore a desirable trait on finer instruments.

Frayed string   A frayed string occurs when the outer metal winding has been worn away by extended use, exposing the round inner core. Frayed strings no longer produce a reliable tone, and can cause injury to the player's fingertips; they should be replaced immediately.

French bow   Referring to a bow's design, not its country of origin, French Bows are the standard model for violins, violas, and cellos. They are played with an overhand grip, and feature a smaller frog than German Bows, which are played with an underhand grip, and are preferred by some Bass players. Both French and German bows are equally acceptable and widely used among professional bass players; the decision comes down to player preference.

Frog   The rectangular part of the bow which anchors and tightens one end of the hair, and over which the player's hand is draped. Finer bows will most often have an ebony frog with a round mother-of-pearl insert; student model bows will often have a molded plastic frog.

German bow   Referring to a bow's design, not its country of origin, German Bows are sometimes used by bass players. As opposed to the French Bow, a German bow has a larger frog, and is played with an underhand grip. Both French and German bows are equally acceptable and widely used among professional bass players; the decision comes down to player preference.

Glasser   A popular student model of mass-produced bow, commonly used by beginning players in school orchestra programs

Glaesel   A popular student model of mass-produced violin, viola, cello, or bass, commonly used by beginning players in school orchestra programs. The other two are Knilling and Scherl and Roth.

Graphite   The "lead" found in number two pencils, useful for fixing slipping or stuck pegs (the graphite is applied to the holes in the peg box, as well as to the part of the shaft of the peg that contacts the hole).

Grip   The cushiony material (usually leather or vinyl) wrapped around the shaft of the bow near the frog, on which the player's thumb rests. Also known as "bow grip" or "thumb grip," the grip prevents the player's thumb from slipping out of place, and protects the bow from damage caused by the player's thumbnail digging into the wood. Worn grips should be replaced immediately.

Guarneri   A family of string instrument makers from Seventeenth and Eighteenth Century Cremona, whose instruments – along with those of Stradivarius and Amati – are highly prized for their superlative tone quality.

Hair   The stringed fibers (often real horsehair, though synthetic materials may be found on student model bows) which, combined with rosin, create the friction necessary to vibrate the strings and produce sound. Violin, viola, and cello players generally prefer white hair, while bass players sometimes opt for black hair, which is coarser and provides more grip for thicker strings. Bow hair should never be touched, as oils from the skin will attract dirt and prevent the hair from holding rosin. As a novelty item, bow hairs are sold in nearly every color of the rainbow, though colored hair is generally not acceptable in professional playing environments, and one must be careful when buying colored hair that it is of good quality, and contains only non-bleach dyes.

Hand-carved instrument   An instrument with a hand-carved body (as opposed to machine-made or factory-made) generally denotes higher quality workmanship, use of traditional materials such as maple or spruce (as opposed to cheaper laminates or plywood), and greater attention to detail. The accessory parts (bridge, pegs, fingerboard, tailpiece) on hand-carved instruments are often of a similar high quality.

Humidity   The amount of moisture in the air. String instruments are optimally stored at a constant 30% to 55% humidity, and should be kept away from radiators and hot air vents. Extremely high or low humidity, or rapidly changing humidity can severely damage an instrument, causing cracks, open seams, and other costly repairs.

Humidifier   A device that regulates the amount of humidity in the air (see *humidity* above).

Hybrid Bass   A bass made of a combination of both real wood (spruce or maple) and laminate or plywood material.

Knilling   A popular student model of mass-produced violin, viola, cello, or bass, commonly used by beginning players in school orchestra programs.

Loop end string   The type of string which attaches to a one-prong fine tuner, and is most commonly used as the highest string on violins and violas (as opposed to ball end strings, which are either threaded through the tailpiece or attached to a two-prong fine tuner).

Laminate/Plywood   A low-cost material used in the manufacture of student quality instruments suitable for beginning level players (as opposed to the more expensive spruce and maple found on fine instruments).

Lower bout   The outside curves on the lower half of the string instrument's body located below the C bout on either side.

Luthier   A string instrument maker, often able to repair instruments as well.

Machine head   The geared metal tuning mechanism (found on basses only) attached to the side of the scroll at the top of the instrument. The four machine heads on a bass are analogous to the four ebony pegs found on violins, violas, and cellos.

Machine-made instrument   A machine-made body (as opposed to hand-made) generally denotes lower quality workmanship, use of less expensive materials such as laminates or plywood (as opposed to the traditional maple or spruce), and less attention to detail. The accessory parts (bridge, pegs, fingerboard, and tailpiece) on machine made instruments are often of a similar low quality.

Mounting Screw   The top screw of a fine tuner, which a player turns to adjust the pitch (clockwise to raise the pitch, counter-clockwise to lower the pitch). See also *fine tuner.*

Mute   A device attached to the bridge to dampen the sound. Performance mutes are relatively lightweight, and alter the character of the sound, making it pleasingly darker and softer; composers usually direct the player to use a mute with the Italian term *con sordino*. Practice mutes are relatively heavy, dramatically reduce the sound of the instrument, and are generally not used in performance.

Neck   The long, slender, durable piece of semicircular wood which attaches to the bottom of the fingerboard, and extends the strings from the body of the instrument to the scroll. The player's hand is most often positioned on the neck when playing, and the neck is the most appropriate place to grasp an instrument when picking it up (as opposed to grabbing the body).

Nut   A block of wood with four notches (one for each string), located between the fingerboard and the pegbox. The nut raises the strings off of the fingerboard so that they can vibrate freely.

Open Seam   A repair need, denoting any unsealed gap between the side and face (top) of the instrument or the side and back (bottom) of the instrument. Open seams can only be re-glued by a qualified luthier.

Pegs   The small black knobs protruding from the peg box (near the scroll) on which the strings are wound. These are used to tune the instrument by tightening and loosening the string tension. They must be pushed in towards the peg box when tuning in order for friction to hold them in place.

Peg box   A hollowed out space carved in the front of the scroll, which creates space for the pegs and for the winding up of excess string length. Holes are drilled into the side of the peg box for pegs to be inserted.

Peg dope   A semi-soft (crayon-like) material that is rubbed onto the peg shaft to fix slipping or stuck pegs.

Peg hole   The round holes drilled in the sides of the peg box through which the pegs are inserted.

Perfection Pegs   A patented tuning peg, sold by the Knilling Corporation, which looks like a traditional friction-based ebony peg, but which houses an internal system of planetary gears, allowing much more precise and slip-free tuning of the instrument. Perfection pegs must be fitted to an instrument by a qualified string repair technician.

Pernambuco   One of the two types of wood used to make high quality bows for string instruments. The other is Brazilwood.

Plane the fingerboard   To remove dents and grooves from the fingerboard caused over time by depressing the string in the same place over and over. Eventually, a qualified string professional will need to scrape the fingerboard back flat to restore accuracy and playability.

Purfling   The thin inlaid wooden lines which outline the top of the body, and sometimes the back as well. Besides being decorative, purfling reinforces the wood and enriches the instrument's tone. Student model instruments often have either no purfling, or fake "painted on" purfling.

Refit pegs   A procedure to optimize the fit between the pegs and the pegholes – often involving smoothing out the peg shafts and/or drilling out the peg holes – which is required when severe peg slipping or sticking cannot be corrected by peg dope or graphite. This should only be done by a qualified string repairman.

Rehair   A procedure to replace worn out bow hair. Bows should be rehaired every one to two years, more often under conditions of heavy use. In the case of some inexpensive beginner level bows with fiberglass hair, replacing the bow may be more cost effective than rehairing.

Ribs   The sides of the body, located between and perpendicular to the front and back of the instrument.

Rockstop   A rubber-backed disc or rectangle placed on the floor into which cellists and basses place their endpin to prevent the instrument from sliding away while playing.

Rosin   A sticky block of processed tree sap which is applied to the bow hair to improve grip and friction, resulting in crisper articulation and a more rich tone. Unrosined new bow hair will create no sound. Higher quality rosins produce richer tones, and variations among characteristics of various brands of professional grade rosins are a matter of individual player preference.

Set-up   Refers to the fitting of the bridge, fingerboard, nut, sound post and pegs to a specific instrument such that optimal tone and playability are achieved. New instruments require professional set-up performed by a qualified string repair technician before they can be played, and all instruments require occasional maintenance to keep things in proper adjustment.

Scroll   The elaborately curled wood at the end of the neck, which houses the pegs and peg box.

Scherl & Roth   A popular student model of mass-produced violin, viola, cello, or bass, commonly used by beginning players in some school orchestra programs.

Shoulder pad   An adjustable attachment (also called a "shoulder rest") for the backs of violins and violas designed to help the player mold their shoulder and collar bone to the contours of the instrument, helping support the weight of the instrument and prevent sliding around while playing.

Sordino   A device attached to the bridge to dampen the sound. Performance mutes are relatively lightweight, and alter the character of the sound, making it pleasingly darker and softer; composers usually direct the player to use a mute with the Italian term *con sordino*.

Practice mutes are relatively heavy, dramatically reduce the sound of the instrument, and are generally not used in performance.

Sound post   The wooden dowel wedged inside the body between the top and back, beneath the left bridge foot, which provides structural support to the top of the instrument and transfers sound vibrations from the bridge to the body. If the sound post falls, all four strings must immediately be loosened to prevent irreparable damage.

Stick   The narrow concave shaft of the bow between the frog and tip usually made of wood, carbon fiber, or fiberglass.

Stradivarius   A family of string instrument makers from seventeenth and eighteenth century Cremona, whose instruments – along with those of Guarneri and Amati – are highly prized for their superlative tone quality. Beware: many copies of these exist with fraudulent labels that confuse consumers.

Strings   The four round "wires" stretched at high tension between the tailpiece and the pegs, which vibrate to produce sound when bowed or plucked. Most modern strings consist of a gut, synthetic, or steel core which is spiral-wrapped or sheathed in metal.

Stripped   Condition when the threading of the screw on endpins, fine tuners, or chin rests will no longer grip the grooves of the base properly to hold it in place, most often caused by overuse or abuse. Stripped items should be replaced.

Tailpiece   The tapered piece of black ebony, plastic, or other wood, located just behind the bridge at the bottom of the body, which anchors the strings to the end button or end pin. Fine tuners, if present, are attached to the tailpiece.

Tiger striping   The striped woodgrain pattern found on the back of higher-quality instruments (as opposed to the shiny, monochromatic finish found on student model instruments). Although the effect is purely decorative, skillfully aligned flaming is often indicative of higher quality workmanship, and is therefore a desirable trait on finer instruments.

Tip   The delicately curved upper end of the bow stick, usually trimmed in ivory, bone, or silver. Plastic tips are common on student model bows.

Unraveling string   A frayed string on which the outer metal winding has been worn away by extended use, exposing the round inner core. Frayed strings no longer produce a reliable tone, and can cause injury to the player's fingertips; they should be replaced immediately.

Upper Bout   The outside curves on the upper half of the string instrument's body located above the C bout on either side.

Varnish   The decorative finish applied to the top, back, and ribs, which protects the wood of the body and affects tone color. Varnish should only be applied by a qualified professional. To polish the varnish, use only specially designed string instrument polishes; never use water or furniture polish.

Violin shop   A business that sells and repairs string instruments. Most shops sell all four instruments of the string family, not just violins.

VSO   "Violin Shaped Object" The derogatory term string teachers apply to a cheap instrument whose too-good-to-be-true price tag initially seems like a bargain, but whose inferior materials and workmanship often result in repair and set-up costs greatly exceeding the value of the instrument. Buyer beware!

Warped   A bow stick is warped if, when sighting down the stick from frog to tip, there is a pronounced curve to the left or right (the stick should remain largely centered over the hair). Warped sticks are most commonly caused by overtightening or by failing to loosen a bow when done playing.

Winding   The decorative wrapping around the bow stick just above the frog and grip. Winding helps protect the bow, and also can be used by skilled bow makers to adjust the balance point of the stick.

Workmanship   The build quality of an instrument including the fitting of the bridge, fingerboard, nut, sound post and pegs to a specific instrument such that optimal tone and playability are achieved.

Instrument Use Contract

Name _____   Instrument _____

Make/Model _____   Serial Number _____

Shoulder Pad/Rockstop (yes or no) _____   Rosin _____

Soft Cloth *(I will provide this for myself and use it at each class/practice session)*

List any problems/defects: _____

Please, initial each of the following and then sign below.

_____ (initial) I will bring the instrument to all performances and rehearsals as requested and demonstrate appropriate care and maintenance procedures including:

- *wiping off rosin and fingerprints after each use*
- *loosening the bow after each use and never touching the bow hair*
- *careful handling of instrument and accessories to prevent breaking*
- *keeping the cello/bass endpin in at all times when not playing (even if just setting it down for a second)*
- *packing, unpacking, and storing it in the case properly*

_____ (initial) I understand that instruments are expensive to repair or replace and that is suggested that these instruments stay on campus except for approved experiences. I will maintain the instrument in its current condition and understand that ***I am financially responsible for any and all damages that may occur to it while it is in my possession.*** A hold will be placed on my records until these are paid.

_____ (initial) I understand the instrument must be transported with care including knowledge of the following:

- *It cannot get wet.*
- *It cannot be subjected to extreme heat or left in a car.*
- *It cannot be transported via bicycle, scooter, motorcycle or any other method likely to cause damage. to the instrument.*
- *Damage resulting from inappropriate transport or negligence will make me fully liable for the replacement cost of the instrument.*

_____ (initial) I will play only the instrument assigned to me and will not allow anyone else to play the instrument assigned to me.

_____ (initial) I will not allow others access to keys to instrument storage closets, and *I will not leave the instrument unsecured at any time*. I understand that leaving instrument storage unlocked makes me liable for any and all instruments left open to theft or damage due to my actions.

_____   _____

Signature   Date

61

String Instrument and Storage Set-Up

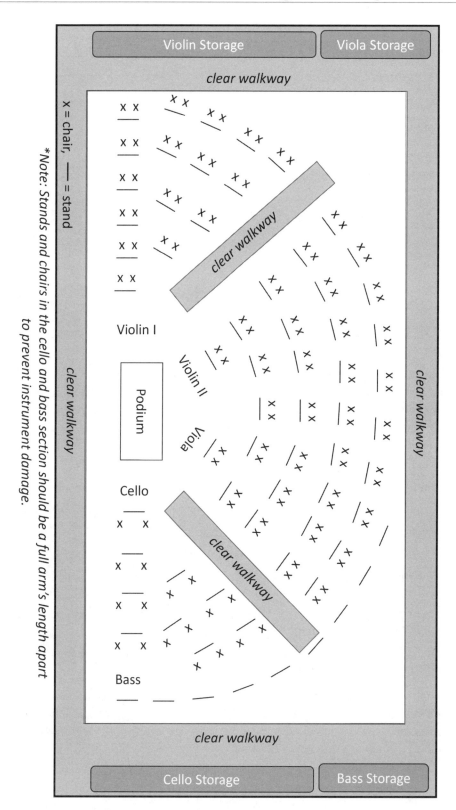

Violin Storage

Viola Storage

clear walkway

x = chair, —— = stand

*Note: Stands and chairs in the cello and bass section should be a full arm's length apart to prevent instrument damage.

clear walkway

Violin I

Violin II

Podium

Viola

Cello

clear walkway

Bass

clear walkway

clear walkway

Cello Storage

Bass Storage

ABOUT THE AUTHOR

Sandy Goldie teaches undergraduate and graduate music education courses at Virginia Commonwealth University in Richmond, Virginia, where she is the string music education specialist and Assistant Professor of Music Education. Before moving to Richmond, Dr. Goldie taught string music education courses at the University of Florida where she completed her PhD and was awarded the David Wilmot Prize for Excellence in Music Education. She received her Master's Degree in Music Education from the University of Georgia and her Bachelor's degree in instrumental music education and performance from the University of South Carolina.

Dr. Goldie has presented her music education research and pedagogy ideas at state, national and international conferences including the International Society for Assessment in Music Education, National Association for Music Education, American String Teachers Association, The Midwest Clinic, Society for Music Teacher Education, and State Music Education Association Conferences in Texas, Florida, Georgia, South Carolina, and Virginia. She has worked to promote music education at the local, state and national levels through leadership positions in professional organizations such as the *American String Teachers Association* (former state president of the South Carolina Chapter, current President-Elect of the Virginia Chapter and Chair of the College Committee), *South Carolina Music Educators Association* (former executive board member of the orchestra division), *Virginia Music Educators Association* (State Collegiate Advisor working with NAfME chapters across the state of Virginia), *American Viola Society* (President-Elect of South Carolina Chapter and Executive Board member of the Virginia Chapter). Dr. Goldie also serves on local Arts Advisory Councils and works with area schools who serve disadvantaged and at-risk students to help provide access to string instruments and instruction.

Dr. Goldie is an active conductor/clinician, professional performer (violist), and advocate for music education. She enjoys working with young musicians throughout the United States and has conducted many honors groups, all-region orchestras, district clinics, youth orchestras, as well as the 2009 South Carolina All-State Orchestra. She has enjoyed working with students of all ages in the public schools as an orchestra teacher for fourteen years. Her school orchestras have consistently received superior ratings each year at state performance festivals in South Carolina, Georgia and throughout the United States and abroad, performing in places like Hawaii (1st Place High School Orchestra Division), Italy (2007 tour of Rome, Venice, Cremona and Florence), Orlando, Williamsburg, Myrtle Beach, Atlanta, and New York. Her orchestras have also routinely performed in local nursing homes and elementary schools in order to share the joy of music and music education with others in the community. She has performed professionally with symphonies in South Carolina, North Carolina, and Georgia (South Carolina Philharmonic, Charleston Symphony, Charlotte Philharmonic, Symphony Orchestra Augusta, and others). Today, her greatest loves are her family, her dog (Murray), her new cat (Charlie) and the joy of sharing the excitement of great music teaching and performing with her students and fellow teachers.